SEASONS OF A LEADER'S LIFE

Muriithi Wanjau

SEASONS OF A LEADER'S LIFE
Copyright @ Muriithi Wanjau, 2019
Published by Fearless Influencers Ltd
P.O. Box 27584-00506, Nairobi, Kenya
Email: info@mavunochurch.com
Tel: 254 720051763

ISBN: 978-9966-8218-9-8

Editing by: Rosslyn Mutahi, rosslyn@toptier.co.ke, +254 720 758617

Cover picture: by Art Creative Ltd, www.artcreativeltd.com, 0706243297

Design layout & Print: by Blackrain, www.blackrainltd.com, 0723212812

DEDICATION

To Carol, my better half, my God-given opposite and equal, who helped me shape the ideas in this book.

CONTENTS

INTRODUCTION

The idea of the stages of a leader's life came to me during a meeting with one of my leadership mentors, Gerald Macharia. He is a brilliant thinker, with a mind that is able to cut through complex issues and get to the core of a matter. In our then regular coffee meetings, I would pour out some of the challenges I was facing; raising leaders and leading a growing church, and then would listen raptly and take notes as he gave refreshingly different perspectives from his experience in the banking and non-profit world. I always came away from those times refreshed! I still don't remember what question I asked that day, but I remember Gerald mentioning how he planned his life in ten-year segments. At that time, he was CEO of a bank, but he intended, after doing that for ten years, to transition to a mentor role to the new CEO and to chair the bank's charitable foundation. For some reason at that time, I was extremely intrigued by this idea. It was one of those thoughts that absolutely capture your imagination and refuse to let go!

I was at a personal retreat soon after when I came to the realization that this had definitely been a divine conversation. As I took a prayer walk at that retreat, I received a very clear picture in my mind of what the seasons of my leadership journey going forward would be. What was even more fascinating is that the names of the seasons even rhymed. I need to put in a disclaimer here and say that that is not something I experience often! When I got back to my room, I quickly wrote them down and began to pray about them. The different stages as I conceived them then are...

- Foundation stage (0-10 years) – an extremely important time when you learn from home;
- Education stage (10-25 years) – the season when you learn from school, peers and society;
- Preparation stage (25-35 years) – the season when you must understand yourself;
- Production stage (35-45 years) – the season when you must set up your impact platform and economic engine;
- Propagation stage (45-55 years) – the season when you cement your legacy by empowering younger leaders who will ensure it lives beyond you;
- Representation stage (55-65 years) – the season when you leverage your networks and resources to ensure that your successors succeed; and
- Reflection (65+ years) – the season when, as a sage, you primarily influence the vision by sharing wisdom with others.

My wife Carol, who trained as a marriage and family therapist, played a big role in helping me think through these stages. She introduced me to psychologist Eric Erikson's stages of psychosocial development, which were helpful as I continued to research the seasons of a leader's life. I have also been since exposed to the teaching of Bobby Clinton, one of my professors at Fuller Theological Seminary, who wrote extensively about stages of leadership development. I have cited both works in the endnotes.

The idea behind these seasons is not to prescribe where you should be in life or to put you in a box. They are not meant to induce guilt or put anyone under pressure! Rather, they are a guide, helping you to intentionally think through and plan for your purpose journey and your contribution to the world. The suggested timelines for each season may be different from person to person. As you read about the different seasons however, you may recognize some important milestones that you successfully accomplished and understand how they are helping you in your journey today. You may also spot some that you completely missed, and hopefully begin to see how to institute them into your life, to ensure you don't leave out an important piece of your leadership foundation.

It is in the only Psalm attributed to Moses, one of the greatest leaders who ever lived, that we find these powerful words, *'Teach us how short our life is, so that we may become wise!'*. When we have clarity about what we should be doing at each season of our leadership journey, we are then able to move with focus and effectiveness to complete the appropriate tasks for that season and to prepare for the next. It's about doing the right thing for the right time.

I hope you'll find these seasons as useful as I have on my own leadership journey. And that they will play a part in helping you become the leader that you were created to be!

Muriithi Wanjau

1 *Psalm 90:12, Good News Bible*

FOUNDATION
Starting off Right

Let me begin with a question. What would you do if you won two hundred and fifty thousand dollars? What's the first thing you'd buy if you found yourself rolling in unexpected cash? I did a little informal interview with several people about the first thing they would spend money on, and I discovered several popular options. Do you identify with any of these fictitious people?

a. **"Pimp-My-Life Polly":** You believe in style so you would immediately give your home, wardrobe and/or car a much-needed facelift and perhaps take a nice vacation to a dream destination.

b. **"Prison Break" Paul:** You would immediately quit your job, settle your debts and look forward to telling everyone who's been making your life miserable to 'keep the change'!

c. **"Sensible" Sammy:** You would mostly think about investing in real estate or shares, and perhaps putting aside college funds for your kids.

d. **"Mother Theresa Tina":** Your first thought would be how excited you are to tithe to your church and then to bless many people and solve many problems in society with your winnings.

So, which of the above seem most appealing to you?

Now that you have indulged in that delightful fantasy, let me gently bring you back to earth. Millionaire lotteries abound today. Some are said to be making a hundred thousand dollars a day. But did you know that most lottery winners end up broke several years later and even worse off than before? Their afflictions include divorce, drug addiction, depression and violence by or against them.

Many have actually said they wished they had never won the money! Several years back, Kenyan media carried a story about Miriam, a seventeen year old who won a Mercedes Benz worth 650,000 dollars. Almost immediately, her life exploded when her mom showed up and accused her common-law husband of living with an underage girl. After that, Miriam disappeared. It turns out her relatives kidnapped her and hid her in a remote region, under house arrest! She escaped several months later and was reunited with her lover. Her family then came over to say they were sorry for their bad behavior. Not long after, she and her husband ended up in court; she left him to focus on her studies. And two years later, she was completely broke and regretted winning the money. Sometimes life truly sounds like a soap opera!

Now, of course you're thinking, 'I'm sure I would be different'. But are you really, truly certain?

When we look around in life, we realize that some of the opportunities we wish we had have actually destroyed others. A little while back, I learnt about the fate of one of my high school classmates who I really admired back in the day because of his nice toys. He came from an extremely wealthy family. Many of my friends got pocket money of around 80 shillings each term, which was around 80 US cents. I did say it was a while back!

But this guy got 1000 shillings (around 10 dollars). To give context, this was almost the same amount as our per term school fees! His dad dropped him off in a cool car and because of guys like him, I sometimes told my dad when he brought me to school in his pickup truck, to drop me outside the school gate so I could exercise by walking the rest of the way. Truth to tell, I was rather embarrassed to be seen in that old pickup! Well, despite all that, my classmate was later jailed for fraud and ended up dying from alcoholism before he turned forty.

Perhaps you too have admired friends who were wealthy and thought, 'If I had what they had, I would be much happier!' Or you've looked at those who were extremely beautiful or amazingly handsome and said, "If I looked like that, my life would be different!" Or you've known people who were academically brilliant and thought, "If only I had a mind like that, life would be so stress-free!"

The problem with that type of thinking is that true success is not something that can be given to you. It has to be developed. If you were not already living a successful life before the 'big break' came, that opportunity you're praying for could lead to your destruction! And so, the best way to prepare for success is not to hope or pray or hustle for that lucky break, but to take the time to build the type of foundation that will support a successful life. And that's why, in this book, we want to begin by looking at what foundations we should be laying at the different seasons of our lives in order to position ourselves for lasting, all-rounded success. Not just financial, but in all other areas as well – spiritual, emotional, physical and relational.

So, let's begin by looking at the foundational years, which are from birth to age ten. Why is it important that you understand this stage well? Well, if you are a parent, this will hopefully give you some great parenting insights. If you're not a parent, you may be able to glean nuggets that help you to positively influence your nephews and nieces and perhaps your own children, if you do become a parent one day. But most importantly, you need to understand this important season because your foundation in those early years greatly affects your readiness to succeed today. I suspect you may discover things in this chapter that were missed out in that early season of your life that are negatively affecting your leadership today.

Focus On Academics Or Values?

The focus of many parents in the foundation years is helping their children succeed academically. In our culture, this has to do with ensuring they get into a good school and pass their exams! At the end of every year, newspaper and TV channels carry pictures of the children who scored the highest marks in the national primary and secondary school exams. Often, they're carried shoulder high by proud relatives and neighbors who are rejoicing at the child's performance. And in our grades-obsessed culture, it's not surprising to see young children carrying heavy bags to school and doing homework every night of the week. Our philosophy seems to be, 'if you can succeed at school, you will succeed in life.'

But while academic excellence is a good thing, it is often a case of placing the cart before the horse. Can you think of someone who had high grades and maybe even multiple degrees, but ended up a failure in life? I can think of many! While education is important, the primary emphasis in the first decade of a child's life should be on building a foundation of values. What are values? Values are an internal set of standards that govern who a person is and how they behave. Teaching your child the right values will help them work well with others, succeed in relationships, including marriage and become good citizens who contribute towards the wellbeing of the society. This foundation sets them up for future success. And whichever way money or fame comes their way – through hard work or sudden windfall – they will be able to receive it graciously and use it to achieve their purpose and make a contribution to their world.

King Solomon, a great leader who was also the richest and wisest man in his day had this to say…

> *A good name is to be chosen rather than great riches, loving favor rather than silver and gold.*
> *The rich and the poor have this in common, the LORD is the maker of them all.*
> *A prudent man foresees evil and hides himself, but the simple pass on and are punished.*
> *By humility and the fear of the LORD, are riches and honor and life.*
> *Thorns and snares are in the way of the perverse; he who guards his soul will be far from them.*
> *Train up a child in the way he should go, and when he is old he will not depart from it[2].*

According to Solomon, it's not luck a child need to succeed in life, it's training! What are the things you should have learnt at this season? For you parents, what are some of the things you need to train your children in? I spoke with several parenting coaches and asked them which are the three most important values a child must learn in this season. To my surprise, their

2 *Proverbs 22:1-6 NKJV*

list agreed with one that my wife Carol and I had drawn up. These values are embedded in the passage we read.

Three of the most important values that a child should learn at this season are obedience, delayed gratification and responsibility.

1. Obedience

According to Solomon, *'by humility and the fear of the Lord, are riches and honor and life'*[3]. In other words, a life of submission and obedience to God will in result in God-defined success, defined here as 'wealth and honor and life'.

When Carol and I were still dating, we visited some friends who had a very strong-willed toddler. She used to throw tantrums and kick such a fuss that it was difficult to believe she was so small! As we were talking to her dad, he took something from her fingers that she wasn't supposed to be playing with.

We braced ourselves for the inevitable and sure enough, she contorted her face and began to demand it back. But then something happened that I've never forgotten. Her dad looked at her directly and without raising his voice, firmly said 'No!' Immediately, the little girl quieted down and stopped the fuss. It was like magic! Fascinated, we asked the dad what the secret was. He told us that he and his wife had attended a parenting class and in the process had learnt how to discipline their child in a biblical way. At that point, we immediately resolved that when we got married, we would do the same class! Sure enough, a few years later when our firstborn daughter was not yet a year old, we took the class. I can confidently say that class changed

3 Proverbs 22:4 NKJV

our lives! It taught us how to parent in such a way that we have greatly enjoyed being parents. And today, when we see parents who have multiple well-behaved young children, we don't say 'how lucky they are!' We know that it doesn't take luck; it takes training!

The amazing thing about kids is that you don't have to teach them how to do wrong. Whether it's taking something that's not theirs, telling a lie or being mean and selfish to others, it comes naturally! All children are born strong-willed and will always push their boundaries. Most parents respond in one of two ways. The more traditional response is punishment. We do what we saw our parents do; which is unleash pain with a belt or slippers or any other means necessary! But the bible talks about training, not punishment. On the other extreme are parents who, influenced by modern psychology and their own negative experiences growing up, don't want to discipline their kids. So, they instead practice indulgence, giving their kids whatever they want and trying to love them into compliance. None of these is a biblical (or effective) approach!

It's important to understand that all children are born disorganized. Solomon also taught that *'folly is bound up in the heart of a child'4*. It is the parent's job to organize them by setting boundaries for them. That's what it means to 'train up a child'. Unfortunately, most parents today end up taking up the disorganization of their kids into their lives. They feel it is inevitable that a home with young children should be loud, untidy, stressful and chaotic. But this means they are allowing their children to train them, instead of the other way round!

4 *Proverbs 22:15*

So, how early should we start to train up a child? By eight or nine months, a child can tell the difference between right and wrong. Even at that age, you can start teaching your child gently that they need to respond in obedience to your authority, rather than doing whatever they feel like doing. This is one of the most helpful things to understand at this age and will help them later in their relationships with their spouse, boss, fellow employees and friends.

So, how are you doing in the area of obedience? Please rate yourself with the following self assessment questions. Remember to be as honest as you can. You're not doing this to impress anyone, but to remove the obstacles that keep you from becoming the leader that you were created to be!

Rate yourself on a scale of 1 (absolutely not) to 5 (very true about me!)

- Do you find that you struggle with authority?

- Do you find it easy to kiss up to those above you, but look down on or ignore those who work for you or are your subordinates?

- Do you find it hard to listen to instructions and to accept consequences?

- Do people find you hard to lead and resist having you on their team?

If you found yourself with a high score, this is probably a symptom of a foundation that wasn't built solidly in your life and needs attention, before it sabotages you.

2. Delayed Gratification

A second important value to teach in this season is delayed gratification. Kids need to learn that everything should be taken

in moderation and in its proper time. They should not always get what they want immediately. We learnt this from our good friends who would take their children with them to business meetings. They would expect the child to keep themselves occupied quietly until the meeting was done, and this was not by handing them an electronic gadget! Delayed gratification sets the basis for discipline and self-control. As King Solomon said in the passage we read earlier, '*Thorns and snares are in the way of the perverse; he who guards his soul will be far from them* ⁵'. A person who knows how to control himself or herself can steer clear from the obstacles that come in the way. A wicked person is defined as one who has no ability to guard his or her soul. Through learning self-control, a child is able to delay gratification in order to cut through all obstacles and get where they need to go.

So, how are you doing in the area of delayed gratification? Please rate yourself on a scale of 1 (absolutely not) to 5 (very true about me!)

- Do you struggle with lust, sexual promiscuity or marital unfaithfulness?
- Do you struggle with different addictions like alcohol, food or drugs?
- Do you find it extremely difficult to save money, or to stick to a budget?

---

5 Proverbs 22:5

- Do you find it hard to stick to a routine or to live a disciplined life?

High scores may point to cracks in your foundation that can destroy your ability to succeed.

3. Responsibility

The last value is responsibility. People who live and act responsibly gain a reputation and a good name. In the passage we read, King Solomon taught, '*A good name is more desirable than great riches; to be esteemed is better than silver or gold*'[6]

Children are born naturally selfish and self-centered. They must be taught to think of others first and to use what they have to benefit others. By two years old, children should be able to tidy up and learn how not to write on walls. You shouldn't have to move things away so they don't destroy them! By age four to six, they should be assisting in the chores like setting the table, clearing and washing dishes and sweeping the house. They should be learning how to bathe and dress themselves.

They should be learning to take care of their property and that of others, and how to make their beds.

For example, at a young age, our kids learnt to wash the dishes and to cook. By age ten, they could cook family meals and each was washing their own clothes. They took turns washing the car. I'll never forget how one of our neighbors called us to talk to us about one of our girls, who had been invited to her daughter's birthday party. She was thoroughly impressed because, before going to play outside, our daughter had noticed the dishes piled up in the kitchen and had decided to clean them

6 Proverbs 22:1

up. When our neighbor came into her kitchen, she was so amazed to find it spick and span that she was calling to ask if she could give her a money gift to show her appreciation! Needless to say, we were very proud parents. Our kids got invited to many parties at this age because parents loved their influence on younger kids. Their grandparents also enjoyed

having them over to visit, as did many of our friends.

Can I be honest with you? The reality is that there are some parents that many people hesitate to invite to their homes, especially if it means they bring their children with them! They are tiring to be around and you have to prepare yourself mentally before you host them, including putting away anything of value, because it will be broken if you don't. The parents look by helplessly as their children run amok and say it's because they're sleepy or some other reason. These parents find it difficult to leave anyone with their children if they need to travel, even for one night. But they've come to see this behavior as normal for little children. They figure it's only for a season anyway. But here's the chilling fact; whatever behavior you see in your cute three-year-old, please project it to when they'll be twenty because they won't magically grow out of it. What seems 'cute' today will one day be irresponsible and anti-social behavior that could land them in a lot of trouble!

And that's why Solomon warned, *'A prudent person foresees danger and takes precautions. The simpleton goes blindly on and suffers the consequences'* [7]. Don't be a simpleton of a parent! It's definitely easier to indulge your children and allow them to be irresponsible, but the result will be punishment for both you and them in years to come.

19

So, how are you doing in the area of responsibility? Please rate yourself on a scale of 1 (absolutely not) to 5 (very true about me!)

- Do you struggle with being dependable and reliable?
- Do people find it hard to trust you to deliver a job well, or are people reluctant to trust you with their resources?
- Does your spouse complain that they carry all the weight in your marriage?
- Do you find it hard to keep a job despite being more than qualified for it?
- Do you constantly find yourself jumping from project to project and not quite finishing well?

If you find yourself scoring high on these, it could be a symptom of cracks in your foundation that need repair.

Other Values

There are other values like honesty, modesty, kindness and generosity that are also important. Of course, all these values need to be taught in a context of love and acceptance. Children's lives at this age rotate around their parents. When our kids were that age, we were their heroes and could do little wrong in their eyes! This gave us a huge opportunity as parents to create in our home an atmosphere of love and acceptance in which we could teach them values. When children feel accepted and loved by their primary caregivers, they develop confidence and a healthy self-esteem.

Why is it so difficult for parent's to set the right foundation in this season?

1. Ignorance

Most people either parent the way they saw their parents do it or they try to do the opposite of what they saw them do, which leads to reactive parenting. Unfortunately, parenting is one of those things most people don't go to school for and yet it is something that affects them for generations to come! For example, I find it sad that some fathers prioritize other things over attending our church's parenting class, and send their wives instead, not understanding that fathers have the largest responsibility to play in parenting.

2. Busyness

A second reason many parents fail to set the right foundation for their children is busyness. At the time most people have young children, they are also working hard to succeed at their careers. Thus, many have little time to spend with their children and the children end up being brought up primarily by house-helps and teachers. The harassed parents often feel so guilty that they try to pay for the time they're away by showering their children with gadgets and gifts. Children are let loose to watch what they want and to sleep when they want.

The new normal is that instead of organizing our kids, we end up accepting their disorganization for ourselves. But this is to their future detriment. The modern myth that we must be all that we can be doesn't work! If you want well-rounded kids, you will have to make some sacrifices in your own career advancement. When our children were younger, we realized we were both way too busy and that our lifestyles were unsustainable. I was leading a growing church and Carol was running two very demanding businesses. We hardly had time

7 Proverbs 27:12 (NLT)

for each other, let alone the kids! So, we made the difficult decision to sell both businesses and live on one salary. Carol stayed home for two years with the children and only gradually started re-engaging with work once they were settled in school. Of course, this meant lowering our lifestyle expectations and not advancing as fast financially as we may have wished, but we have never regretted that decision for one minute!

Remember, when it comes to setting a good foundation, it's not luck you need, it's training.

Let me conclude this chapter with three possible application points. What can you do if for one reason or the other, you have a cracked values' foundation? You basically have to undo the negative values and relearn positive ones. You have to retrain yourself. Whether it's how to honor authority in your life, how to be generous, kind, truthful or self controlled, or how to become a responsible person. This process of retraining is called discipleship. At Mavuno, we have a training process called the Transformation Loop. It begins with a ten-week class called Mizizi (Kiswahili for 'roots') that begins to point you to your purpose. It puts you in the context of a group of people who can keep you accountable and help you become who God is calling you to be. The idea is to move from being a self-centered indulgent consumer to an other-centered community-impacting agent.

It's a great way to begin the journey of discipleship as an adult!

If you are a parent, I would challenge you to think through what it would mean to limit your own career or social advancement for the sake of being present to instill values in your children. For those who are married, this includes being present for your spouse, as a stable home is one of the best heritages you can leave to your children. I would also encourage you to explore taking a biblically-based parenting course. Being equipped to be a good parent is one of the best ways to ensure future success for your children.

In the next chapter, we'll look at the second season, ages 11-25, and see what critical things we must learn from it to succeed.

EDUCATION
Building Support Systems

The year was 1994. The date was September 22nd. A hugely popular show was launched in the US. The concept was six young people in their twenties, living on their own and struggling to survive in the real world. But they found that the companionship, comfort and support they got from each other was the ideal solution to the pressures of life. The show was "Friends" and it became a huge success during its ten-year run, during which all the members of the cast achieved household celebrity status, not just in the US, but in 100 countries across the world. Its DVD sets continue to sell millions of copies worldwide. The show won 63 different awards, including six Emmys, one of the highest awards a TV show can get. The final episode of the show was watched by an estimated US audience of 51.1 million [8].

Why did this show become such a huge hit? I believe it exposed the hunger that young people today have for close, trusting friendships with others; people who care for us and have our best interests at heart, and in many ways, that's what Friends was about. On the other hand, these friendships though depicted as funny and authentic, had many serious flaws. They were over-sexualized, became dysfunctional, led to broken marriages and resulted in much pain and stress. They say that art reflects life and this show showed the reality of many friendships formed by young adults today.

8 Source: Wikipedia

In this chapter, we want to look at the second important season of life, the years of education, when one is aged between 11-25. If you are at this stage in life, this will be very useful to you. If you have children in this stage, you will hopefully get some helpful ideas. If you are past this stage, I trust that you will still see areas where there may be cracks in your life that you can begin to address.

The educational years are a recent addition to a person's development and are a direct result of the modern education system. This stage was non-existent before colonialism because prior to that time, children would go through a rite of passage and transition directly into adults. If they were men, they would become warriors or protectors of the family. If they were women, they would be prepared for marriage to start their own families. Very similarly in the West, the whole concept of teenager didn't exist before the Industrial Revolution. But today, these 'teen' and 'young adult' years are seen as an intermediate stage when a person is not a child anymore, but still doesn't carry a clear adult role in society. For some, this stage ends early because they take on a job straight after high school, but for many, it lasts till after college.

In this season, several huge changes are taking place in a person's life.

1. Physical and Emotional Changes

As we enter adolescence, we begin to form a sexual identity. This is an awkward stage where boys break their voices and become physically clumsy due to rapid growth. On the other hand, girls begin their menstrual cycles and go through hormonal changes that may cause them to become moody and withdrawn. All this can lead to a very confusing time for the person and for their parents!

2. Independent Thinking

People in this season begin to want a degree of independence to experiment and to test out their own theories about life, as they're establishing a sense of identity. In many cases, this is the season where people begin to push against traditional boundaries, expressed through dress styles, body markings, music, chaotic rooms and so on. Teenagers also begin the process of deciding on their future career direction and sometimes, parents want to have a decisive voice in that decision, just like they've had on other important decisions previously. As you can imagine, this can result in an emotionally intense and stressful season.

3. Self Consciousness

In this season, people want to fit in and to be accepted by or be popular among their peers. That's why high school boys will roll up their school uniform sleeves, turn up their collars and walk with a bounce. Their greatest discovery at this stage is cologne! Girls spend a lot of time in front of a mirror, engrossed with looking good. Even as you enter the twenties, this self-consciousness and wanting to be seen a certain way by others remains very important.

4. Peer Influence

Young people in this season no longer see their parents as all knowing or all powerful, and often have developed other relationships that they now consider as wiser and more 'with it'. Because of their desire to fit in and gain acceptance, many teens experiment with the things that their peers are engaged in, including drugs, sex and watching porn. I remember drinking irresponsibly during my high school years despite the fact that I hated the taste of beer, simply because I felt it was a way to fit belong with the 'in' crowd!

All these things are happening when the person is in school, and the push from home is on getting good grades, going to a good college and getting a good degree. Many parents have no idea what challenges their teens or young adults are going through. And so, they either continue treating them as children or they give up and allow them to experiment without guidance. Some parents even try hard to be their children's peer. Unfortunately, none of these parenting approaches help them to win in life!

What are the lessons that a person should learn through the educational years? There are several, including how to handle money wisely. It is not uncommon when we travel abroad to see young Kenyan students racking up thousands of dollars in credit-card debt, and then spending years out of college trying to pay it off. All they had learnt about money in school and at home was irrelevant to help them succeed in the adult world! Sports and academics are also important at this age, not necessarily because they'll help the person make money in the future, but because they'll teach them the disciplines of hard work and focus.

However, because the influence of peers is so important, by far, one of the most important lessons to learn is to teach your teens and to learn for yourself as an adult how to form and maintain positive friendships. We said in the last chapter that if you won the lottery and didn't have a foundation of values, it would actually destroy your life. What we're saying here is if you succeed in your career, but don't have a wall of solid and dependable friends around you, it will leave you even more isolated and lonely, surrounded by sycophants who don't care for you. That is a recipe for failure in life!

King Solomon, the wisest and richest man of his generation, wrote an entire book to pass on wisdom to a young man in this season of life. One of the themes it emphasizes greatly is that of positive relationships. Here is one such example.

Wounds from a friend can be trusted, but an enemy multiplies kisses. He who is full loathes honey, but to the hungry even what is bitter tastes sweet. Like a bird that strays from its nest is a man who strays from his home. Perfume and incense bring joy to the heart, and the pleasantness of one's friend springs from his earnest counsel. Do not forsake your friend and the friend of your father, and do not go to your brother's house when disaster strikes you – better a neighbor nearby than a brother far away [9].

Our passage shows us some of the qualities you need to look for in a positive friendship, as well as some of the qualities you need to have if you are to be such a friend to others. There are at least three tests here...

1. The Realness Test

As Solomon said, '*Wounds from a friend can be trusted, but an enemy multiplies kisses. He who is full loathes honey, but to the hungry even what is bitter tastes sweet*'[10].

I went to an all-boys high school that prided itself on teaching you how to be a man. Apart from the academics, there was a

9 Proverbs 27:6-10 (paraphrased)
10 Proverbs 27:6-7

great emphasis on competitive sports. Another popular pastime was

'debates' with girls' schools. Our debating club would visit different girls' schools, ostensibly to debate various important current issues. Our main agenda however, was learning how to charm and impress girls as a necessary lifeskill! Now all these activities were valuable. Sports and academics helped me learn to focus and to push myself to work hard. The debates helped to demystify the opposite sex.

But this socialization also created some major problems for me. It taught me to view relationships with ladies as sexual and relationships with guys as competitive. In other words, we learnt how to make superficial relationships because we were constantly projecting an image. You couldn't let your guard down! One result for me was that for years, I found it easier to relate to women than to other men. I was good friends with many girls, some of whom I could share deep concerns with, but despite being on sports teams and having many male friends, I didn't confide in any of them!

One day, my pastor challenged me. He'd watched me take out a girl from church for dinner one week and then a different one the next week. When he asked my intentions, I said they were both just friends. He looked me straight in the eye and said, 'Muriithi, there are some men who lead men, and there are some men who chase women. Choose which one you want to be!' Ouch! I made the decision there and then to change how I related to women, but it took me many years to learn to make good, healthy friendships with other men. In a way, it's a lesson I'm still learning!

Who are your friends? This passage is saying that you should learn to make friends with people who can be real with you and with whom you do not have to maintain a certain image. People who will speak the truth in love to you. People who are not impressed by your reputation – not 'fans' who only tell you what you want to hear. Who are your friends? Are you able to speak the truth in love to them? Do they feel free to ask you the hard questions about life? Do you find yourself only able to share deeply with people of the opposite sex? Do you find it hard to form good, healthy friendships with people of the same gender? These are all signs that your walls are broken and need repair. The second test for positive friendships is…

2. The Value-Add Test

King Solomon continues, *'Like a bird that strays from its nest is a man who strays from his home 11. Perfume and incense bring joy to the heart, and the pleasantness of one's friend springs from his earnest counsel'*. This quality has to do with value-addition. Do your friends reinforce positive values in your life or do they cause you to misbehave? Are you a better person when you are with them? As King Solomon's father, David also taught, *'Blessed is the man who does not walk in the counsel of the wicked or stand in the way of sinners or sit in the seat of mockers.12*

Who are your friends? This passage says, rather than seeking to surround ourselves with people who are cool or popular, we should instead surround ourselves with people who help us become better people. Along the highway to God's purpose, you'll need travel companions who are headed in the same direction. These are the friends who share your values; who

11 Proverbs 27:8-9
12 Psalm 1:1

believe the same things about reality that you do. You will need friends who will help you resist the pressure of individualism and materialism in the media.

For example, if you believe that time with your wife and family comes before career advancement or personal entertainment, it's difficult to walk the distance with friends who have the opposite values. This is what happens to many men. Your friends start making fun of you at the office: 'this guy is always running home after work. He must have a curfew!' Next thing you know, it's after work and there you are, going for a drink with the guys. Many of those guys have terrible relationships with their wives. In no time at all, your relationship with your family has become secondary and neglected. Somebody once said, 'show me your friends and I'll show you your future.' You become who you hang out with!

For parents, one thing you can do in this regard is put your children in touch with other children who share their values. When our girls were younger, my wife came together with several moms of girls who are around the same age. They began a monthly meeting with their daughters with the intention of not only helping these girls understand their sexuality, but also helping them become best friends with others who have the same values. I also remember that when I was a teenager, my parents allowed us to invite our school friends over, and where possible, they also befriended their parents. My parents are people of deep faith and through their influence, several such parents were influenced to become people of faith as well! Through their example, my parents were teaching us to influence our peers positively. King Solomon said elsewhere, '*As iron sharpens iron, a friend sharpens a friend*'[13]. Value-adding friends are friends

13 *Proverbs 27:17*

that improve each other's lives. The third test for positive friendships is...

3. The Commitment Test

There are those friends who give you a lot of airtime when you're doing well. They enjoy your company and are generally available to you and even seek you out. But when things are not going well, you would never think of sharing about it with them because your relationship only goes so far. Jesus also had such people around him. They wanted to be around him because he was getting famous. According to the report of one of his followers, John, *'many believed in him as they saw the miracles he performed. But Jesus did not trust himself to them, because he knew what was in their hearts'*[14.] While he didn't chase them away, he knew the difference between a fan and a true friend. And he had such friends. In his darkest hour, Jesus was able to be real with them; to share his deepest fears, to cry in their presence and display how hard it was for him to face the cross.

So, once more, who are your friends? Do you have friends who are committed to you no matter what? Who will stay by your side in good times or in bad? Who you know you can call when things are not going well and you can count on them to make sacrifices on your behalf? Do you have friends who can count on you in the same way?

If not, then it's a great sign that your walls are damaged and in need of repair. In King Solomon's words, *"Do not forsake your friend and the friend of your father, and do not go to your brother's house when disaster strikes you – better a neighbor nearby than a brother far away"*[15.]

14 *John 2:23 (GNB)*
15 *Proverbs 27:10*

32

The key lesson in your teen and young adult years needs to be building positive friendships. If you didn't learn to build such

friendships, your walls are in disrepair. You are in danger of setting yourself up for loneliness and sexualized and competitive relationships, which are unhealthy and very unfulfilling. You are in danger of settling for unreal or virtual relationships; today, many find it easier to relate virtually on social media than to real people in real life! Even in marriage, you're in danger of not knowing how to be friends with your spouse. You'll need outside stimulation and entertainment to keep your relationship together as you won't know how sit and connect closely with another human being.

In today's competitive marketplace where there is an abundance of people with academic qualifications, what will set you apart is not your grades or degrees but your emotional intelligence, the ability to work will with people and have people work well with you. And so ultimately, regardless of how much money you make, if you can't make positive friends, you are in danger of setting yourself up for life-failure!

It's never too late to begin to repair this foundation. I met a man in his sixties recently who told me that a few years ago, he and his wife realized they needed real friends. They had built a successful business, but along the way, they realized that the friends they had were really business colleagues and social acquaintances and not the companions they needed for their purpose journey. And so they began to pray for God to bring such companions their way and also to posture themselves differently in order to find such friends. They followed King Solomon's advice that *'a person who wants friends must himself be friendly'*[16] and so began to create time for positive friendships. God had answered their prayers and at the time we were speaking, they had become very close friends with several younger couples who had similar values and were moving in the same direction. This man shared how this had positively impacted, not just his marriage, but his faith and his sense of excitement about the future.

Along your journey to purpose, there will be many discouragements and reasons to give up. The only way to ensure you make it is to surround yourself with friends who are real with you, who add value to your life, and who are committed to you no matter what; who don't just know your professional life, or your social life, but know all your life; who are heading in the same direction that you are. Maybe you have friends that are real and authentic with you, but you realize that they don't add positive value to your life, influencing you instead to do things you know are not right. It's time to evaluate your friendships and to intentionally surround yourself with friends who share a similar mission and values. You owe it to yourself to surround yourself with such friends!

16 Proverbs 18:24

PREPARATION

Setting Clear Direction

So far, in the past two chapters, we've discussed the first two seasons of a leader's life and the tasks you must engage in during the first part of your life as a young person.

Education 11-25 (Students): **Positive Friends**
Foundation 0-10 (**Child values**)

In this chapter, we want to move on to the next season, which is the years of preparation. These typically happen today when a person is between 25 to 35 years of age. In ancient times, the years of preparation began as soon as one went through a rite of passage and moved from childhood into adulthood. But when the modern school system added an intermediate education stage, then they were pushed for many into the early 20's after person graduated from college. In our context, this is the first time that many have their first real experience of adult independence. These tend to be optimistic years. The whole world is ahead; you look forward to a good job or lucrative business, a quick rise up the career ladder, a fat bank account, opportunities to travel, and of course, the perfect spouse and kids! This season is defined by several factors.

1. Self Determination

When you were a child in your parent's home or a young adult in college, someone else made the rules. But at this stage, many leave the sheltered environment of the home or the college dorm and are now responsible over the huge and important decisions that affect life direction such as career, where to live, what lifestyle to maintain and so on.

2. Career Launch

At this stage, you finally enter the 'real world' of productive work. You join the workforce and begin providing for yourself. This can be a tough and demanding assignment. However, some end up making a whole lot more money than their parents ever dreamt about!

3. Long-Term Relationships

Many get into serious relationships, get married and begin families. This means that the friendships you form in this stage usually have great impact for good or bad on whom you end up becoming in life.

Even though it's an optimistic time, it can also be a challenging time. One of the biggest challenges is impatience. There's a feeling that you're young once and this is it! When I was 24, one of my mentors was 40 years old and I remember thinking how ancient that sounded. To me, it felt he had one foot in the grave! As a result of their impatience and short-term perspective, people in this age tend to face certain pressures...

1. Pressure to Succeed and Maintain a Certain Image

There is high pressure to succeed in this stage. This could be based on several factors...

- Your parent's lifestyle. Many want to instantly have the same, if not a better lifestyle than their parents have, disregarding the fact that it took those parents many years to get to where they are;

- A desire to escape a life of poverty. Some face expectations to support their siblings' education and upkeep, as well as the parents who educated them as a 'retirement plan'.

- The pressure to keep up with peers. I remember one of my friends visiting Carol and I with his new Range Rover. He wanted us to thank God for it and say a prayer for it and in his excitement, he asked me to sit in the driver's seat and press the start button. All I remember is smelling the leather seats, hearing the muted roar of the powerful engine and thinking, 'Oh God, what am I doing with my life!' As different friends begin to succeed financially, it puts a pressure on people in this life stage to compete and also have the same 'toys'.

All this results in pressure to make a lot of money and to make it fast. To drive a fast car, live at a posh address, work for a prestigious company, do an MBA with a well-known university and so on. Everyone's doing evening and weekend classes to add to their qualifications; everyone's engaging in side hustles to add to their income. It feels like a race to the top and if we stop running, we'll get left behind!

2. Pressure to Marry and Have Children

This is especially true for the ladies. In the early to mid twenties, a few of your peers get married before finishing or just after college. But with time, this trickle turns into a flood. You're constantly attending weddings! By the time you're in late twenties, your friends start trying to hook you up and your parents start asking your aunties to talk to you. By your early thirties, you meet with your friends and they're all talking about babies, so you feel out of place. As a result of this pressure, many rush into relationships with the wrong person or before they are ready and end up divorced or as single parents.

3. Career Confusion

Many in this season did certain college degrees because their parents pressured them to or because they looked prestigious at the time. But when they join the workforce, they realize this is not what they want to do. Others find themselves paralyzed. They are so gifted and could excel in many different things, but don't know which one to focus on. A few manage to make a lot of money fast and find themselves facing 'quarter life crisis' and wondering, 'is this all there is to life?' The result is a generation drifting from one opportunity to another, uncertain about what they should be focusing on and afraid that they're missing out on living out their potential.

What are the lessons a person should be learning in these years? Although there are several, I believe the most important one is discovering your purpose. Just like we said about the other building blocks, even if you do extremely well financially, but do not answer the important questions, 'who am I?' and 'what am I here for?', you will eventually find your success empty and without meaning. King Solomon also had some select things to say about this topic. For the rest of this chapter, I'd like us to reflect on the following quote by him.

What do workers gain from their toil? I have seen the burden God has laid on the human race. He has made everything beautiful in its time. He has also set eternity in the human heart; yet no one can fathom what God has done from beginning to end. I know that there is nothing better for people than to be happy and to do good while they live. That each of them may eat and drink, and find satisfaction in all their toil—this is the gift of God. I know that everything God does will endure forever; nothing can be added to it and nothing taken from it. God does it so that people will fear him [17].

Let's face it, 'purpose' is a rather over-used word today! So, what is purpose really? This passage talks about the 'burden God has laid on the human race'. Burden in this passage means a heavy responsibility, occupation or task. According to the bible, every human being comes to earth with a pre-assigned responsibility or task, designed for them by the Creator. And even though it comes with responsibility, discovering your purpose is extremely beneficial. Our passage talks about four benefits of living in your purpose...

1. Purpose Motivates

Speaking about the Creator, King Solomon says, *'He has made everything beautiful in its time'*[18]. Life can get hard. Sometimes you face discouragements and setbacks. Purpose provides the motivation to keep going, knowing that somehow, as long as you are aligned to the purpose God created you for, what you are doing will result in beauty in its time. Everyone loves seeing a champion winning a trophy – the lights, the reporters, the acclaim. But the hidden part of that victory is training every day, rain or shine, whether your body feels like it or not!

Most of life is not as glamorous as it seems from a distance. But purpose gives significance to the otherwise meaningless or painful or frustrating details of our lives. This was true about

17 Ecclesiastes 3:9-14
18 *Ecclesiastes 3:11*

Jesus, of whom it is written that he, *'for the joy set before him...*
endured the cross' [19]. Because he knew the big picture, Jesus
was able to persevere through the shame and pain of a Roman
execution to achieve His purpose. You need to have a purpose
that is big enough to live for, suffer for and if necessary, to die
for! And even when the inevitable challenges of life come, you
will have a reason to keep going until you overcome.

2. Purpose Directs

King Solomon continues, *'He has also set eternity in the human*
heart; yet no one can fathom what God has done from beginning
to end' [20]. The picture I get here is of these amazing eternal
beings called humans who have no idea what they are capable
for. And as a result, they drift about, clueless of their true
identity. You see, life is a journey and every journey has a
destination. Everybody ends up somewhere in life. But not
everyone gets there on purpose. They say if you don't know
where you're going, then any road will take you there. A clear
purpose provides a road map that removes distractions and
simplifies decision-making.

People without clear purpose are easily distracted. They are led
by opportunity: If I get a job offer that pays more than this one,
I move! And so they are thus constantly drifting from one
opportunity to the next, living for the now and not building
anything of lasting value. At the end of their lives, there is no
clear thing they are known for that will outlast them. Living out
your purpose helps you to say 'no' to opportunities that will
distract you from your life journey, even exciting opportunities!

19 Hebrews12:2
20 Ecclesiastes 3:11

3. Purpose Brings Satisfaction

King Solomon also says, '*I know that there is nothing better for people than to be happy and to do good while they live. That each of them may eat and drink, and find satisfaction in all their toil—this is the gift of God* [21].' Purpose has to do with doing good, making a difference for others. This is the road to true happiness. According to a Harvard study, only 6.7% of the world's population has a bachelor's degree![22] You belong to a truly privileged minority and to whom much is given, much is required! You were created to do good for others. And God intends that your doing good will result in great satisfaction and meaning for you and in the process, provide for your needs.

4. Purpose Gives Meaning

King Solomon concludes, '*I know that everything God does will endure forever; nothing can be added to it and nothing taken from it. God does it so that people will fear him.*' [23] Like our Creator, we create meaning through our work and should engage in work that has eternal value. A clear purpose, with the courage to follow it through, dramatically increases your chances of coming to the end of your life, looking back with a deep abiding satisfaction and thinking, "I did it. I succeeded. I finished my race well. God received maximum glory from me. My life counted for something!" This is what drove the apostle Paul to write in his old age, '*I have fought the good fight, I have finished the race, I have kept the faith. Now there is in store for me the crown of righteousness, which the LORD, the righteous Judge, will award to me on that day—and not only to me, but also to all who have longed for his appearing*' [24].

21 *Ecclesiastes 3:12-13*
22 *https://www.huffpost.com/entry/percent-of-world-with-col_n_581807*
23 *Ecclesiastes 3:14*
24 *2 Timothy 4:7-8*

Living out your purpose is living out who you were created to be. It is living for eternity. This is what God created you for – you are an eternal being! You were created to contribute something that is bigger than you to society, something that will outlast you: Something that counts towards God's eternal purpose. Without a clear purpose, the odds are that you will come to the end of your life wondering whether you really lived up to your potential. And if your life really mattered at all.

Clearly, the most important thing you can do in this season is to figure out your direction before you set off on it! Many rush in to make riches first. They send out a hundred resumes after college and take the first good job that comes along. They figure out which business hustle will make the most money and go for it. But if you're supposed to be going to Kisumu and you discover you're on a bus to Mombasa, going faster won't get you there! You have to get off, get back to Nairobi, and then pick the right bus to Kisumu. Only then can you get to your intended destination. What I'm saying in this chapter is, before setting off on your journey, know where you're going! And that friends, has to do with your purpose.

Now, it would be unfair to end this chapter without exploring one last question. How do you go about discovering your God-given purpose? There certainly is no formula to this and the most significant thing I can encourage you to do is be faithful to serve God where He has placed you. In the process of doing so, I believe He will reveal to you just why He created you!

But along with that, here are a few things you want to build into your life to help you on this journey...

1. Know God

To discover your purpose, it's important to know the Author of that purpose. As King Solomon reminded us, it is God who has set eternal purpose in our hearts. You need to move from letting others define you and begin to let your Creator to define you. There is no shortcut for this! Just like with any other relationship, we only grow our friendship with someone by spending time with them. We know God by learning to regularly read and meditate on His word, which is one of the main ways He speaks to us today. We also spend time in prayer, which is how we communicate with God. And just like any other relationship, the more we spend time with God, the more our minds become renewed and the more we become aware of His desires and preferences. Maybe you've found yourself too busy to do this, but remember – if you're going the wrong direction, going faster won't get you there! I'm not talking about a religious quest here, but a vital exercise for every human being.

2. Know Yourself

Self-discovery means starting to become aware of your passions, strengths and opportunities.

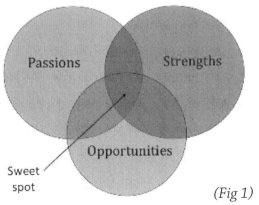

(Fig 1)

'Passion' refers to the things you are excited about. These are those things that you love to do and could even do for free. It could also refer to those things that make you angry, and you wish someone could do something about them. The interesting thing is that not everyone else gets mad about the same things! These could be indicators to you about something that you were uniquely wired to do.

'Strength' refers to the fact that we all have something that we are exceptionally good at. Maybe you're good at public speaking or a great listener. Or you're great at hospitality or you're good with kids. Perhaps you're a natural musician, or good at art, or you're a good farmer and whatever you plant, grows. Explore your strengths and ask those who know you well what they think you are good at. Again, these could be great clues towards how you are uniquely shaped to bless others.

'Opportunity' asks where can I add the greatest value? This area has to do with what societal problems exist around you that you can uniquely solve with your passions and strengths. What are those places of need or brokenness around you – at work, in your family or in your neighborhood and beyond – which you have noticed? Are there some that you can begin to provide solutions for and to bless others? You see, purpose is all about making a difference for others!

Across (fig 2) are a few common situations people find themselves in and some possible remedies.

The idea is to work towards a place where you are spending the largest amount of time doing things that you are both passionate about and strong in and that add value to the world. Don't just

IF YOUR SITUATION IS...	CAN RESULT IN...	HOW TO REMEDY
Strength + Opportunity - Passion	Boredom	Try to figure out how to bring your areas of passion into your current assignment or, if impossible, find another job or volunteer somewhere where you can develop your area of passion
Passion + Opportunity - Strength	Mediocrity	Invest in developing the skills you need, for example, go to school, read widely or do an apprenticeship
Passion + Strength - Opportunity	Frustration	Volunteer somewhere that will give you a chance to develop in your areas of interest, for example, a community organization, a ministry at church, etc.

(Fig 2)

jump from job to job looking for the one that pays the most or carries the most prestige.

This is a short cut to significant midlife crisis! It makes a lot more sense to understand yourself and then to find a way to get paid doing what you love and could even do for free. When this happens, you'll love your job! You'll find yourself saying, 'thank God it's Monday!' instead of 'oh God, it's Monday', which is much more common.

3. Locate Your Mentors

One of my favorite sayings is, 'if you want to see far, don't just jump up and down; stand on the shoulders of giants'. It's of huge important in this season to put yourself in situations where you are mentored by people who are where you want to be. Not just people who are experts in the field you are passionate about, but also those who have values that you admire. Not just people who are financially successful, but people who are all-round successful, including in their marriage, parenting and spiritual life. Such people become the giants whose shoulders you step on and who propel you beyond your peers. I've had the awesome privilege to be influenced by great mentors; people who showed me, rather than just taught me, what I know about how to be a good husband, father, leader and pastor.

But here's one thing you'll quickly realize; the best mentors are busy people! So, how do you get them to be wiling to be around you enough so you can learn from them? As a young leader, I learnt that one of the best ways to get close to good mentors was to find a way to serve them. So, Carol and I would offer to baby sit their kids or look for other ways we could be a blessing to them. Or we would serve in the same ministry at church that they served in or were passionate about. In addition to the mentors that I've interacted personally with, I have also been mentored by others that I've never met by reading their books. I know I would not be who I am today if not for my mentors.

4. Become An Apprentice

One of the easiest ways to be mentored in this season is to learn to serve another person's vision. This is what was traditionally known as 'apprenticeship'. Rather than rush off to start your own thing, slow down and spend some time learning from an older leader. Great leaders throughout history have developed their convictions through serving in someone else's vision. Even though Moses knew he was called to bring deliverance for the people of Israel, he learnt to look after sheep at the feet of his father-in-law, Jethro for forty years in the wilderness before stepping into leadership. Who knew that God was preparing him to lead a clueless, sheep-like mass of people through that same wilderness for the next forty years?

David followed the mad king, Saul, faithfully for almost fifteen years, even though he knew God had chosen him to be the next king. In the process, he learnt how not to be a king. Sometimes your serving someone else's vision will show you how not to do it when it's your turn!

Serving someone else's vision might mean you get rich slower. It will probably mean you simplify your expectations and lifestyle. But better to do it now than to have to stoop down later. At this age, don't be afraid to try out different things. Don't lock yourself in too early by saying, 'I only do this kind of work'. You're too young to know all your strengths yet! Many people find it hard to believe that the thing I hated and struggled with most about being a pastor in the early days was public speaking. And yet today, that's one of the things many people know me for! I would never have discovered it if my mentor had not assigned me speaking opportunities. So, go on, volunteer to help in your church. Give time to a children's home or youth shelter. Do an internship at one or several organizations. Don't be in such a hurry to set off on your career journey before you've established where you want to go!

There is a unique solution that you were created to bring to earth. This is what you want to figure out during your season of preparation. Every one of us was created to be an entrepreneur or an 'intrapreneur'. An entrepreneur is someone who creates solutions while working in their own business or organization. An intrapreneur is someone who creates solutions while employed in someone else's business or organization. This is important to understand. Even if you work as a professional in a company, you need to discover your unique 'sweet spot' and work at it and become so good at it that people will be willing to pay you for your solution!

Now, what if you're a little older and already on a bus, but you are not sure it's going in the right direction? Please note that I'm not saying you quit your job! I'm saying though that it's not too late to engage in the process of discovering your unique purpose. This quest might eventually move you away from your current career trajectory. You might find that your current assignment is actually sabotaging your purpose. If that is the case, I will be the first to urge you to take the courageous step of getting off that bus and looking for one going in the right direction. Many times however, what you need to do is adjust how you see yourself and the value that you bring to your current organization, even before you figure out if you need to step into something else. I would also like to encourage you with the thought that in this journey of following God's purpose, nothing is wasted. God is able to take even the mistakes, fumbles, dark times and 'wilderness' experiences of our past and turn them into resources to effect your eternal purpose. Trust Him!

PRODUCTION
Narrowing It Down

So far, we've looked at the three initial seasons in a leader's life from birth to thirty five years of age. Each of these seasons is a stepping-stone. Without values, it's hard to build the right friends. Without positive friends, even if I discover my purpose, I won't have the support I need to succeed!

| Preparation 25-35 (Apprentice): Purpose |
| Education 11-25 (Student): Positive Friends |
| Foundations 0-10 (Child): Values |

In this chapter, we want to move on to the next season which is often between 35-45 years. I call these the years of production. For those of you who are not there yet, you'll appreciate this chapter because it will show you where you are going and hopefully, you'll see really clearly why you can't postpone building a good foundation for success. For those of you who are in this season or past it, this chapter might affirm some great decisions that you have already made or alternatively reveal some cracks in your foundation and give you the motivation to go back and repair them.

People in the production season are generally…

1. More Settled

This is not true of everyone of course, but for many, they are a lot more settled than they were in the last season of life. There is a sense for many of having found your place in life and of being more set in your career direction and family situation. You are typically earning more and have a position of prestige and leadership in your community. People at this age also generally tend to be…

2. Highly Productive

Because they're no longer as green in their careers, people in this season are typically more productive and have grown in responsibility and leadership in their organization or business. They tend to have made a name for themselves at work. People begin to seek their opinions or their services because of their work experience. This is true, whether they are a doctor, manager, receptionist or mechanic. Some have by now began to receive great recognition for their success. They are sought after and recognized. For example, when you're feeling generally unwell, you can go to see any doctor, but if you have a serious illness, you typically prefer to see an older doctor who has lots of experience in their area of specialization!

Along with these qualities come several challenges…

1. Busyness

For many, life becomes a whirlwind as they balance the demands of work, social relationships, child rearing and other societal responsibilities. In addition, by now, many have a higher standard of living or a larger family, both of which mean higher financial needs. On the family front, your parents are older and a role reversal is beginning to happen. You begin to join the 'sandwich generation', who are both looking after their children and their parents. Because of busyness, many in this season become isolated from friends and even their spouse and family.

2. Disappointment

Along with busyness comes the realization for many that they may not achieve some of their dreams and that time is running out. Many grapple with the fact that they may never be married, while some are realizing that they may not achieve their financial and lifestyle dreams. Your body weight starts distributing itself in places it's not needed! Some encounter their first major health issues with health scares like high blood pressure, diabetes and cancer. I've noticed that in the nicer gyms, most people working out after March, when the New Year resolutions wear out, are older guys, who are probably there under orders by their doctor!

3. Dissatisfaction

Along with disappointment can come a sense of dissatisfaction or disquiet, both at work and at home. Some may have achieved their dreams, but may be uncertain whether it was worth it, as they encounter the consequences of the other things they neglected in their pursuit, for example, relationships with their spouse and children. Some realize their marriage is less satisfying than what they had anticipated. Some begin to question if they entered the right career. This sense of dissatisfaction can lead to some irrational responses. Some respond to it by working harder. Others would like to make some radical life changes but are too tied to their comfortable jobs. And on the opposite extreme, some, in a bid to recapture their youth, begin to engage in destructive behavior, including sexual affairs. As you can see, this can be a very challenging season!

What are the lessons a person should be learning in these years? Although there are several, I believe the most important one is the lesson of focus. This is why we said in the last chapter that it's critical to discover your purpose earlier on. Because once you settle on your God-ordained direction, the purpose of this season is to set out single-mindedly towards achieving it.

So far, we've heard a lot of wisdom from King Solomon. There is another ancient writer I'd like us to learn from who exemplified a focused life. He was a very accomplished leader who was an expert in law, wisdom, religion and natural sciences. From an early age, he was on top of his game at what he was doing. Then he had a radical experience with God that helped him discover his purpose. Courageously, he got off the bus he was on and started off in a new direction. And years later, this is what he had to write about that season of his life.

"Do you not know that in a race all the runners run, but only one gets the prize? Run in such a way as to get the prize. Everyone who competes in the games goes into strict training. They do it to get a crown that will not last, but we do it to get a crown that will last forever. Therefore I do not run like someone running aimlessly; I do not fight like a boxer beating the air. No, I strike a blow to my body and make it my slave so that after I have preached to others, I myself will not be disqualified for the prize"[25].

25 1Corinthians 9:24-27

Paul had discovered the secret of focus. Focus is when you center in on the God-given purpose for your life. You eliminate everything else in order to attain that which is most important. Did you ever realize that every single person alive has the same amount of time available to them each day? Regardless of how rich or poor, famous or unknown, educated or unlearned, we all have exactly the same amount of time in a day as Nelson Mandela, Mother Theresa or Wangari Maathai.

So, why is it that these people have had such remarkable impact while many of us don't? Let me give you a hint: It's not about gifting! It is true that everyone is better than us at something; it's also true that we are better than everyone else at something! Let me give you another hint: It's not about money! Most of these people did not make impact because they had money, but money followed them because they made impact. A key difference between those who have greatly impacted the world and those who haven't is the power of focus. Somewhere in their personal journey, either by accident or on purpose, these few discovered the advantage of narrowing their focus. As a result, they lived out their purpose.

What keeps many leaders from attaining this level of focus?

1. Tyranny of the Urgent

Paul said we must *'run in such a way as to get the prize'*[26]. Many leaders have not taken the time to define what is truly important. As a result, they run after the urgent things in life – those screaming for attention – and neglect the important ones. The interesting thing is that the truly important things in life rarely scream for attention until it's too late! By the time you realize your kids are total strangers, or your marriage is estranged, or

26 1Corinthians 9:24b

your health is gone, or your faith has grown cold, you'll also realize that it didn't happen suddenly. It happened gradually. And it often costs a lot more to restore these things than you could have imagined! By the time many agree to get marriage counseling, their marriage is a complete mess! Or by the time you're in the gym or hospital trying to repair your health, it often costs a lot more money, time and willpower than you could have bargained for!

You must run in a focused way because whatever your purpose, it will take a healthy body, spirit, and family! These are your 'big rocks'. Living a focused life means scheduling in your 'big rocks' first… There are some things you can't delegate to anyone else. For me, these include being a husband to my wife or father to my kids. It also includes time in prayer and God's word, healthy eating and working out. I start by scheduling these important things in my calendar and then fit everything else in the time left. What are some big rocks you have neglected because you are so busy?

2. Ignorance of Purpose

Paul continues, *'Therefore I do not run like a man running aimlessly; I do not fight like a man beating the air'*[27]. When you don't know your purpose, you don't know what to focus on. It's easy to substitute busyness for effectiveness and to find yourself 'beating the air'. Some people find it difficult to say 'no' because their sense of self-worth demands that they make themselves indispensable to others. They take pride in the fact that they're in great demand and their calendars are brimming with people to see and things to do. The busier they are, the more important they feel. They are addicted to adrenalin and

27 1Corinthians 9:26

so can't even rest. They complain of overwork, but in reality, they would have it no other way!

But there is a difference between being busy and being productive. Most productive people seem to have more, not less, discretionary time than the average person! They control their schedules rather than allowing their schedules to control them. The key to focus is learning to do those things that only they can do and delegate the rest. They learn the magic of saying 'no' to opportunities that are not aligned to their purpose.

So, do you find yourself constantly running and hardly able to keep up with your schedule?

3. Distractions and Time Wasters

Next, Paul says, '*I strike a blow to my body and make it my slave so that after I have preached to others, I myself will not be disqualified for the prize*'[28]. One of the ways the enemy opposes your purpose is to send distractions that will keep you from accomplishing it. What are some of these? There are some appointments, hobbies, relationships and invitations that will compete with your life of purpose. Some of us spend a lot of time on email and Facebook or watching TV. Paul says that rather than being enslaved by your appetites, you must learn to 'beat your body to make it your slave'. In a different instance, Paul also wrote, '*Everything is permissible for me, but not everything is beneficial*' [29]. Many things in life are good, but focus means stripping away even good things so you're left only with the best; that which will help you accomplish your God-given purpose. As theologian Dr. Howard Hendricks wrote, 'the secret of concentration is elimination'. What are some time

28 *1 Corinthians 9:27*
29 *1 Corinthians 6:12*

wasters you must eliminate from your life in order to create time to live a life of purpose?

In our early thirties, Carol and I started two businesses; one in media production and the other in the bridal fair industry. Three years later, after a lot of hard work and investment, the businesses were taking off, beginning to make money, employing a lot of people and creating a brand reputation. Around this same time, we were also starting Mavuno Church. As you can imagine, we were extremely busy! In the middle of that hectic time, it became obvious that things were not going too well between us. We would come home in the evening, put our young children quickly to bed after dinner, pull out our laptops and without speaking much to each other, continue with our day's work. It dawned on us that we had become more of business partners than marriage partners! Things came to a head when one of our parents fell ill and we just did not have the bandwidth between us to manage a crisis. We were juggling too many plates at once!

We realized that if we led both the business and Mavuno, the ultimate cost would be higher to our family than we were willing to pay. Something had to give. So, we made a tough decision. We closed both businesses, after which Carol stayed home for the next two years with our children before joining me at Mavuno, once they were all in school. It meant having a lot less to spend as we were now living on one salary, but it's a decision we've never regretted! Slowing down enabled us to spend more time with each other and with our children in those formative years. It allowed us to figure out what was really important to us as a family. It allowed us to get to the place where we decided what we wanted to focus on growing together. We were able to get some of our big priorities in place and also to figure out how to contribute together towards one thing that we both loved. I believe we are still reaping the benefits of that decision many years later!

What are some of the tasks you must engage on during this stage to help you on your journey?

1. Create Your Solution

This is the season when you build the organization, company, ministry, business, non-profit or professional expertise that will allow you to make a positive contribution to your generation. It should also have an inbuilt economic engine to sustain you and help you meet your financial goals, whether this is through salary, royalties, business income, passive income and so on.

You need to decide if you want to begin a new organization of your own or whether you want to create your solutions within an organization began by someone else. If you've taken the time to explore different pursuits, grown in self-awareness, walked with different mentors and learnt from others through apprenticeship, you have probably figured out what you want to focus on and have also built different competencies and experiences that will help you in this season.

It's important to note that building an organization is hard work! Many people, for example, start a business because they are passionate about a certain industry or product. Or they may have academic qualifications or work experience in that particular area. However, passion and technical knowledge are not enough to run a business. Every entrepreneur needs to have a basic understanding of management, sales, marketing, people management, law, taxation and finance in addition to understanding their particular industry. Most small businesses fail because entrepreneurs underestimate what it takes to build an enterprise. One of the books I heartily recommend for all entrepreneurs is 'The E Myth' by Michael Gerber, which is an extremely helpful and easy-to-read guide for how to set up good systems for your organization.

Narrowing your focus allows you to put in the time to become truly great at what you do. Malcolm Gladwell in his book, 'Outliers', says that it takes roughly 10,000 hours of practice to become truly exceptional at something you are already gifted at and well positioned for!

2. Build Your Team

Every great dream needs a great team! One of the key things you need to build during this time is your leadership pipeline or the system that you will use to train younger leaders. Raising younger leaders for your enterprise will ensure your organization or business outgrows and outlives you. Many startups neglect this important step because the entrepreneur assumes he or she can't afford to pay additional staff. One way around this is to run an internship program. A well-run internship program provides valuable work experience and mentoring opportunities for young people. For the organization, it provides a less expensive way to raise skilled leaders. Even if you are employed and not running your own organization, creating opportunities to mentor younger leaders is a great way to grow in your own leadership and to pass on your values and skills to the next generation of leaders.

My wife and I ran a successful video production company that was able to produce work for up to thirty clients at a time. Our sales and marketing team sourced the clients, our front office team booked their shoots, agreed on timelines and managed payments and our production crews shot and edited the video and photography projects. This whole process was managed with a high degree of excellence, from interaction with clients to final work output. All our employees joined our company as interns and were eventually employed or contracted after successfully concluding their internship program. The internship ensured that our employees shared our organizational vision, values and culture. Internships are not just valuable for businesses though. At the church where I work, almost all our top staff leaders are graduates of our internship program.

It's important to note what an internship program is not. It is not an easy supply of cheap or free labor! A well-run program demands time, structure and input to ensure that the interns are getting value for their time at the organization. The end result though, can be a great homegrown team that will take your organization to the next level.

Do you know the difference between a floodlight and a laser? A floodlight is a large beam of light that lights up the area around it. But take that beam and focus it narrowly and it becomes a laser, which can cut through the hardest diamond. To achieve your God-given purpose, you must be a laser, not a floodlight. If you will commit to the process of understanding your purpose and then focusing all your time and resources on the vehicle that will help you achieve this purpose, then money, resources and opportunities will follow. And true success will be your portion in this life.

The result of laser focus is that you are able to build something during these years of production that impacts others and changes society as you follow God's purpose for you. You become a solution provider. And having created your unique solution, you are then ready to spread it around and impact others beyond your immediate circle. And that's the next season of life that we'll discuss in the following chapter.

PROPAGATION

Spreading the Solution

S o far, we've looked at the first four seasons of a leader's life in order to understand what the key lesson or practice needs to be in each season. The seasons and respective lessons are…

Production 35-45 (Builder):Focus
Preparation 25-35 (Apprentice):Purpose
Education 11-25 (Student):Positive Friends
Foundations 0-10 (Child):Values

In this chapter, we want to look at the next season – the propagation years, which may happen when a person is aged between 45 to 55 years old. This has in the past typically been referred to as the early middle age, although this varies from culture to culture. People in this season generally exhibit…

1. Increased Experience

While younger adults generally excel in the ability to take bigger risks and deal with new and unexpected situations, people in this season have typically gained a lot of insights and understanding through their life experiences. They are able to use this understanding to deal with the problems or situations they come across. Their experience allows them to have a more flexible view of the world and they are able to make compromises, work through areas of disagreement and question the status quo. They are able to rely on experience and common sense as opposed to resorting to book knowledge and raw instinct in making important decisions.

2. Increased Credibility

Along with increased experience comes increased credibility. People at this age are generally seen as more trustworthy and what they say as carrying more authority. Younger people may seek them out for their opinions and advice, especially if they are seen to have made positive achievements at work, in the community or in their family life. They may receive invites to speak or share their experiences at different forums. Or they may find that they have a greater role to play in their extended families, with even their parents asking them for advice.

Along with these qualities come some challenges.

1. Physical Changes

Adults in this season begin to notice that their bodies don't function as effectively as they did previously. This includes decrease in strength, sensation and coordination. People who previously had 20-20 vision may develop farsightedness or nearsightedness or both. Weight gain and hair loss begin to occur. Many men experience a dramatic decrease in libido, while many women begin to experience the symptoms of menopause, such as hot flashes, dizziness, headaches and irritability. People in this season may also experience health scares through emergence of conditions such as hypertension, coronary heart disease, diabetes, arthritis, asthma or strokes. All these can lead to an increasing awareness of one's mortality.

2. Emotional Changes

Along with physical changes, this season, similar to adolescence, is characterized by emotional changes. For men, decrease in testosterone production leads to weaker muscles and recovery time, diminished appetite and an inability to push hard at a specific task for extended periods. Many men in this season also face the realization that they are probably not going to accomplish the things they wanted to achieve in life or be able to correct the mistakes of their youth. Along with this, is the feeling that they are no longer as sexually attractive as they used to be. This can lead to anxiety and even depression.

For women in contrast, menopause may mean greater enjoyment of sex and a desire to express themselves, at the same time that their partner's interest is reducing. This can lead to challenges in the marriage. Women also may experience the societal double standard that older men are perceived as being more established and desirable, while older women are viewed as being past their prime.

All the above changes can lead to a diminished self-esteem and to a midlife crisis, where people try to reassert their masculinity or femininity by engaging in more youthful behavior, dressing in trendy clothes, taking up expensive hobbies or engaging in affairs.

3. Higher Stress

As one enters this season, they may face several stress factors. These include the financial and emotional challenges of raising children, the costs of paying off a mortgage and managing debt, the fear of losing their job, the anxiety and cost of dealing with chronic health conditions and so on. One may experience significant stress at work, especially if they feel they have not made adequate progress, are not paid sufficiently or are underutilized. One may also feel under pressure to compete with younger work colleagues. Unemployment can cause significant anxiety, as one may not be as nimble and easily employable as when they were younger. In addition, those who are over-invested at work may now find themselves lonely and isolated.

Adults at this age also often find themselves caring for their aging and sometimes, ailing parents. This can be demanding and stressful, especially for those who by this season had expected to be enjoying relative freedom as their children became more independent.

What is the most important task a person should be undertaking in these years? Although there are several, I believe the most important one is the lesson of succession, or passing on their legacy. During the production phase, you focus and take the time to construct your solution to the world – the thing that you will be remembered for. And now, during the propagation phase, you move from primarily being a builder to being a mentor, who propagates or spreads this solution through others so that it can have a wider impact beyond you.

Jesus demonstrated this very well by investing in and training twelve men, eleven of whom went on to propagate his message across the world. Fewer people have had greater impact than Jesus has! The startling thing however, is that it is because of his apprentices or disciples that his teachings continue to have impact until today. Very early in his ministry, Jesus identified those that he wanted to continue his legacy. A man named Mark wrote these words about Jesus. *'He appointed twelve that they might be with him and that he might send them out to preach'*[30]. The first thing that strikes me about this passage is that Mark was probably mentored by Peter who had been mentored by Jesus. In other words, he was a third generation follower! Jesus' message not only changed the lives of his disciples, but those disciples also passed on this message to their disciples ad infinitum.

The second thing that grabs my attention is the reasons why Jesus was appointing the twelve. It was not just so that he could send them out as co-workers to preach the gospel. It was also so that 'they might be with him'. In other words, Jesus intentionally was selecting a group of men who he would give almost unlimited access to his time and life. From then on, he would share meals and lodging with them. He would teach them how to pray, but they would also observe him in prayer. He would send them out to heal the sick, but they would also be next to him as he healed. They would see him laugh and they would see him cry and in the process, they would not just learn his message, but they would learn to be like him.

In fact, Jesus' ambition was not just that they would be like him, but that they would be even more effective than him! One of his disciples quoted him saying to his small team, *"Very truly I tell you, whoever believes in me will do the works I have been doing, and they will do even greater things than these, because I am going to the Father"*[31]. What kind of leader says that? A lot of nations in Africa have struggled because many of our presidents

30 Mark 3:14
31 John 14:12

don't want to let go of power. They believe they are the only ones who can lead their nations! And this is true not just in our nations, but in many of our homes and churches as well. Many of our businesses and non-profits suffer from 'founder's syndrome', where the charismatic founder stifles the growth of the organization they began because they are not able to step aside and free others to lead critical functions as the organization grows. But Jesus actually wanted his followers to do far greater things than He Himself did. And because of how he invested in pouring into and preparing them to do so, the work He began as one person two thousand years ago is now carried on by billions of people across the world today!

Great leaders across the world have understood this fact. Jack Welch, former CEO of one of the largest companies in the world said, "Before you are a leader, success is all about growing yourself. When you become a leader, success is all about growing others." Former US president Ronald Reagan said, "The greatest leader is not necessarily the one who does the greatest things. He is the one that gets the people to do the greatest things." I believe the mark of a great leader is not how great their organization is while they are there, but how great it remains after they are gone. Or to put it differently, the true test of a person's leadership is the health of the organization when the organizer is gone.

What is it that keeps many leaders from intentionally raising and passing on their work to successors? Several factors, including...

1. We Don't Want to Feel Dispensable

Many leaders feel that if anyone else can do their job, then perhaps their own contribution won't be appreciated or seen as valuable. And so, they hold their cards close to their chest; which gives them a sense of importance. I sometimes take issue with certain lawyers or doctors because they like to explain your problem in such jargon that you are guaranteed to always need their services! The truth is that none of us like to feel dispensable. For example, many people struggle to write a will. They feel that if they talk about death, it might come sooner!

2. We Don't Want Competition

Many people fear to groom or mentor someone because they might take their job before they are ready to leave! Some people even fear to go on leave from work because the boss might find out they are not the only ones who can do what they do! This really comes from a 'limited pie mentality', which constantly asks, "if I share with others, what will be left for me?"

3. We Don't Want the Hard Work of Succession Planning

The reality is that it takes time and patience to train others. This is time you could be using to do more work! And often, the people you are training won't be able to do the job as well as you anyway, at least at first. Because of this, many leaders prefer to do their role by themselves.

In light of all these obstacles, why should we still go ahead and mentor others so as to raise successors at work, at home and in all our other responsibilities?

1. It Allows For the Growth of the Leader

Mentoring others frees me to start other things. If I hold on to my ministry or work role, I will not be able to begin other initiatives and will remain at the same level. When I bring up my followers to my level however, it frees me to move up and take up another responsibility or get more equipping. It also frees me to focus more on what only I can do well! Many leaders spend 80% of their time doing work that others should be doing and only 20% doing work that only they can do. Mentoring others frees me to reverse that equation and spend 80% of my time doing what only I can do.

2. It Increases the Capacity of the Ministry

As I mentor others and raise multiple leaders, my organization or ministry is able to grow and accomplish more because it has more capable leaders. The leaders I raise may not be more gifted than I am in general, but each of them is more gifted than I am in something. When I free them to lead in their areas of strength, we attain synergy, where our net impact is greater than the sum of our individual contributions. In other words, the organization is not limited to my strengths and limitations.

3. It Ensures the Continuity of My Work

No leader is indispensable. There will always come a time when that leader's gift is not the greatest need of the hour. We all have limitations. Often, God will raise a new leader with less fame and prestige, but with the specific gifts needed to take the organization the next step. Many times a startup organization needs an innovative and entrepreneurial founder who is able to take huge risks to start something people have not seen before. But as the organization grows, the future entrepreneurial leaders should also be good managers, who can manage the complex systems that come with growth.

4. It Gives the Credit Where it Belongs

Mentoring and raising up other leaders recognizes that I am neither eternal nor indispensable! It is a clear statement that whatever responsibility I have, whether it's my job, the organization I lead, or my role in my community or in my family, all these are gifts from God and I am only a steward, looking after them in order to be a blessing to others. As I raise others, I am demonstrating that my mission is greater than me and will outlive me. This brings longevity to whatever it is that I am called to do.

After leading Mavuno for 10 years, I knew my time had come to transition to a new role within the vision. During those years, Mavuno had become a vibrant congregation with a clear mission and vision and one that was effective at doing what we were called to do. We had grown in numbers and income and were no longer seen as a raw startup but had begun to gain respect from the society. At this point, Carol and I began the process of passing on leadership of our largest campus to one of the younger pastors we had trained so that we could focus on mentoring those leading the other churches that we had begun. I won't lie that it was an easy thing to do; in many ways, it was moving away from something we had become very good at and gained much recognition for and moving into a role that had a lot less clarity and visibility. Our role became to coach and raise lead pastors who would now take the more visible role of teaching regularly at their church locations.

In other words, it's our job to ensure they become greater than us. Ouch! I'll be honest, I've had people tell me, "You must be crazy; no one gives up power or responsibility when they're so young!" And truth be told, it's actually not easy to see people you have mentored as leaders now begin to receive the credit and the accolades that I was used to receiving. But here's the thing; as we have made this transition, we have been able to see Mavuno grow from six congregations to today's thirty, scattered in ten different nations! And we are much better positioned than we've ever been to become a movement of culture influencing churches in every capital city of Africa and the gateway cities of the world by 2035. Every time I see one of these pastors do even greater things than me, I'm full of joy. I am excited because this vision will definitely outlive me!

What are some of the tasks you should engage in while in this stage? Here are a few suggestions…

1. Coaching Your Successors

Coaching is coming in vogue nowadays, but few leaders know how to do it well. Most leaders opt for what I call the 'deep end' model of leadership development. You throw them into the deep end and the ones who swim and survive are the ones who were meant to be in this organization! The problem with this model is that it only works with already naturally skilled leaders and is wasteful, letting go of potential leaders who just needed some input to move from common to great. Using the deep end method makes you a people user as opposed to a people developer.

Coaching allows me to grow the person by helping them take responsibility for their decisions. A while back, I learnt six coaching questions from my friend Dave Ferguson[32] that

32 http://www.daveferguson.co/6-coaching-questions-for-developing-leaders.
Alternatively, you could use Marshall Goldsmith's six questions on
https://www.marshallgoldsmith.com/articles/6-questions-for-better-coaching/

became the basis for my monthly individual meetings with my direct reports. The questions are as follows...

1. How are you? This relational question may seem superfluous. However, as someone once said, 'People don't care how much you know, until they know how much you care'[33]. Checking in with your leader by asking how they are doing relationally, physically, mentally or spiritually shows that they are not just a means of production and that you are interested in how they are doing.

2. What's working well for you? This question starts your conversation on a positive note. You will learn some good things about your report and your organization that you might not otherwise have learnt by asking someone what's working well in their role.

3. What challenges are you facing? Here you get to hear the key challenges your report is facing. You need to resist the temptation to give advice and solutions as this will short-circuit their own development and their sense of responsibility! So, listen carefully, take notes and clarify what you heard.

4. How will you tackle these challenges? This is where true coaching happens. By asking the person to define their own solution, you are allowing them to think and grow. Once they speak, you can prompt them with further questions if you feel their answer is insufficient. The idea is to poke holes until they have an idea that has a good chance of succeeding.

5. How can I help you? Sometimes we assume we know what the person needs. When we ask, we demonstrate our respect

33 This quote that has been attributed to many people over the years including President Theodore Roosevelt, John Maxwell and Earl Nightingale.

and desire to understand them and their needs. The answer to this question should also include an element of accountability. For example, 'by when will you have completed this action and how will we assess that it has been successful?'

6. How can I pray for you? Like the first question, I've found that this one communicates my care for the person I'm leading. Praying for your leaders changes your heart, changes your relationship, and changes your leadership.

Coaching ensures that I continue to pass on my values and culture to the organization. Management guru Peter Drucker famously said, 'culture eats strategy for breakfast'. It doesn't matter how brilliant your strategy or vision is, if you have a terrible organizational culture, then you will not attain the best results! Coaching also creates a good team environment by helping me stay relationally connected with my leadership team. In this season, I lead my top leaders more through influence and relationships. With their experience, they can easily choose to work elsewhere and my personal relationship with them is an important factor in keeping them motivated. In addition to meeting them monthly as a team, I also plan coaching meetings with each of my executive team, at least once a month.

2. Provide Alignment

As you begin to share the load of leadership with other strong leaders, you need to ensure the organization remains aligned to one vision. You must ensure that there are good relationships between your top leaders and that they are collaborating and not working in silos. At Mavuno, one of my executive team members is in charge of the alignment function and she works directly with me to ensure that all our departments and campuses are pulling in the same direction.

Have you ever heard of Mordecai Ham? I thought not! So, let me tell you about him. He was an American evangelist who ran a radio broadcast. I know that doesn't help! So here's something else. One of the people who got saved, discipled and launched through his ministry was a young man named Billy Graham. By the time Billy was dying, he had spoken to over 2 billion people through crusades, TV, radio, print and shared the gospel with presidents and kings. Many young people from all over the world were inspired to become involved in the work of sharing the gospel across the world because of Billy Graham. You may never have heard of Mordecai Ham, but you have most likely been influenced by a person who was influenced by him!

It's easy to criticize our government leaders for suffering from founder's syndrome and thinking no one else can lead the nation besides them. But we need to be careful that we ourselves are not guilty of ill-preparing our families or colleagues to succeed and exceed us. Stop and reflect honestly today. If God was to move you somewhere else today, would the work you are doing halt or die completely or would the work of God's kingdom continue unhindered? Are there those you are passing on your skills and knowledge to who are able to continue with the work?

REPRESENTATION
Leveraging Credibility

S o far, we've looked at the first five seasons of a leader's life ...

Propagation 45-55 (Mentor):Share
Production 35-45 (Builder):Focus
Preparation 25-35 (Aprentice): Purpose
Education 11-25 (Student):Positive Friends
Foundation 0-10 (Child):Values

In this chapter, we want to look at the next season – the representation years, which may take place when a person is aged between 55 to 65 years old, or what could be referred to as late middle age. I'm careful with that definition though because even the term 'middle age' is a social construct and means different things in different cultures! People in this season generally exhibit the characteristics of the former season, but in an enhanced or more acute way. They have even greater experience as well as credibility. The good thing with middle age is that you finally have a confluence of strength and wisdom. Younger people often have lots of strength, but lack wisdom because of not having much experience in life. Older people often abound with wisdom but lack the strength to run around and exert themselves to bring positive change to the world. But in the years between 45 and 65, a person is potentially at that pivotal stage where they have gained a good amount of wisdom

and still have strength to leverage that wisdom and bring change.

The challenges of this season are also similar to the ones of the former one, to an enhanced degree. These include the physical changes, emotional changes and stress occasioned by their life stage. Hopefully though, as they get further along into middle age, people begin to get more comfortable with their mortality and limitations and settle down to accept, appreciate and even enjoy their life stage.

There are several tasks that a person in this life season should be engaging in, but an important one is the lesson of leveraging their credibility to resource their vision. During the propagation phase, you move from primarily being a builder to being a mentor and multiplier of builders, which allows your work to have a wider impact beyond you. But during the representation season, you hand off even the work of propagating the vision to others and now leverage your increased credibility to raise resources that will take the vision further and faster than your successors could by themselves.

A person who exemplifies this stage well is the apostle Paul. He was a feared persecutor of Christians who had a dramatic encounter that left him a changed man. From that time on, he dedicated his life to preaching about Jesus to people who did not know about him, especially non-Jews, also known as Gentiles. In the course of several missionary journeys, he began several churches in strategic cities of the Roman world. In each of the churches, he appointed elders to lead the congregation while he moved on to another city. A large part of the biblical

New Testament comprises of letters that he subsequently wrote to those churches, encouraging them in their faith and addressing different questions or issues that they were facing.

When a particularly hard famine greatly affected the church in Jerusalem, which was mostly comprised of Jewish Christians, Paul took it upon himself to challenge the Gentile churches to donate money to support those who were affected. He sent messengers ahead of him to these churches to share the vision so they could be ready to donate generously. He then took the offering from these churches, along with a few representatives from the churches, on a long trip to Jerusalem. For example, he wrote to the church in the city of Corinth,

"Now about the collection for the Lord's people: Do what I told the Galatian churches to do. On the first day of every week, each one of you should set aside a sum of money in keeping with your income, saving it up, so that when I come no collections will have to be made. Then, when I arrive, I will give letters of introduction to the men you approve and send them with your gift to Jerusalem. If it seems advisable for me to go also, they will accompany me"[34].

Several other scriptures describe Paul's encouragements to the Gentile churches to give[35]. In the process, we get the picture of a man who had gained sufficient moral authority among the early Christians that he could challenge them directly about their generosity and they in turn were willing to entrust him with significant resources to convey to Christians in other parts of the world. Because of his track record of integrity and his past

34 1Corinthians 16:1-4
34 For example, 2 Corinthians 8:1–9:15, Romans 15:14–32
35 For example, 2 Corinthians 8:1–9:15, Romans 15:14–32)

track record and results, people were willing to give sacrificially to a cause larger than themselves.

I have witnessed several leaders at this stage, including my mentor, Pastor Oscar Muriu. Over the years, he has given brilliant leadership to a growing movement of churches, raising multiple leaders in the process. The movement of churches he leads, Nairobi Chapel, has good accountability systems and a good reputation for integrity. He is also a wise and insightful leader who has developed a keen sense of discernment and clarity of thought. As a result, he is widely sought after as a speaker, both locally and internationally. Many have seen him as a statesman, and a good representative of the church in Africa. He has been able to lead his team into developing quite a number of church and organizational partnerships and has been able to attract key resources such as money and skilled personnel that have accelerated Nairobi Chapel's vision.

I believe that's what God wants for every leader! What are the things that will stand in the way of your ability to engage well in this season of representation?

1. Lack of Results

This happens if the person fails to apply himself or herself in a focused way to building an organization, vision or skills that will attract people to want to work with them. As a result, they are not known for anything! They have not demonstrated expertise at something or developed tangible results, and so, they are not seen as having a valuable contribution to give outside their organization.

2. Lack of Successors

When you fail to develop and mentor others to do what you do in the previous stages, then you will not be able to take a step ahead, outside the running of the vision, in order to effectively resource the vision. You will be too busy managing the organization! Many leaders in Africa have been leaders for years, doing the same jobs and leading at the same level. They consider leading their organization as the apex of leadership and so they cling on to power and fail to create room for their successors to grow. As a result, the best leaders leave their vision when the opportunity presents itself and they are left surrounded by people who are less gifted. This vicious cycle means that they will never have the capacity to spend sufficient time to figure out how to leverage their credibility outside their organization.

3. Lack of Moral Authority

Leadership is built on trust and credibility. When a leader fails to build these qualities during the course of their leadership, then they will not have the moral authority to leverage for the sake of their vision. You may know of leaders who dented their credibility through a financial or sexual scandal and found it difficult to lead at the same level afterwards. There are also some leaders who pursued success at all costs as they grew their business or organization and stepped on people along the way, as they climbed up the ladder of success. As a result, they are feared and perhaps even admired and respected, but they are not loved or trusted. This may stand in their way when it comes to developing external relationships and partnerships that will accelerate their vision.

What are some of the tasks you must engage in during this stage to help you on your journey?

1. Resource the Vision

By this stage, one of the best gifts you can give to your organization is the credibility that you have accrued and the networks that you have built over the years. The younger leaders you have raised may have more energy than you do and may be able to manage the organization in your absence. You have the ability though to bring resources their way that will help them go faster and further. Such resources include money, connections and people. A leader at this stage should learn how to build external partnerships and how to seek opportunities and resources that could benefit his or her organization. They should seek to build relationships with other leaders, locally and internationally, within and without their industry. They should add value, not just within their organization, but to the wider society beyond. They should also open doors for their top leaders to do the same, with the ultimate aim of connecting the vision with whatever it needs to move to the next level.

2. Work Smart

At this stage, the leader's greatest contribution is from their wisdom and not their energy! Leaders at this stage need to move at a pace that allows them to be of greatest effectiveness. You need to ensure that you set enough time aside for reflection and for key relationships and you need to make your schedule work to enable you to do this. I've seen effective leaders at this stage go to the office only a few times a week, as the rest of the week, they are networking with other leaders, mentoring their next generation leaders and working from home. Instead of traveling across town to attend meetings, they schedule their meetings close to where they live and people come to them. They are in demand as speakers and consultants and they strategically plan time away from their organization to allow younger leaders space to lead and take responsibility.

Carol and I are actively preparing for our season of representation. As we actively mentor our campus pastors and their spouses, our prayer is that they will grow to become great mentors to the next generation of leaders. We want to transition to the place where the movement has great leaders who are capable of growing and expanding it without our direct input. Our role then will primarily be to resource those leaders as they grow the movement, as well as to build external partnerships and to become a resource to the body of Christ beyond Mavuno.

As we've said before, each season of a leader's life builds on the one before it! Failure to build values at an early age or to grow good accountability relationships as a youth or to narrow down and focus on growing a particular vision or skill set could result in a struggle later on, as you seek to leverage your credibility to accelerate your vision.

REFLECTION

Becoming Yoda

S o far, we've looked at the first six seasons of a leader's life. We want to conclude with the seventh; what we call the reflection years. The seasons can thus be represented in this way, with each one building on the one before it.

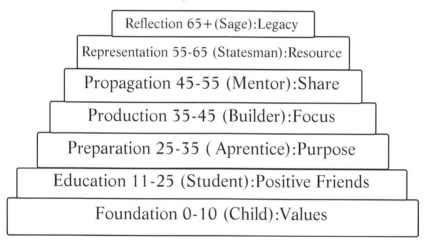

Reflection 65 + (Sage):Legacy

Representation 55-65 (Statesman):Resource

Propagation 45-55 (Mentor):Share

Production 35-45 (Builder):Focus

Preparation 25-35 (Aprentice):Purpose

Education 11-25 (Student):Positive Friends

Foundation 0-10 (Child):Values

The reflection stage can happen when one is aged sixty-five and above, although with medical advances and continued improvements in healthcare, this may vary among individuals and cultures. While you may not yet be in this stage, it's important to understand what it entails, as knowing what's coming up ahead will help you live more intentionally in order to be prepared for it. At this stage, you will be experiencing further changes.

1. Wisdom from Experience

Adults at this age have greater life experience, which usually leads to greater understanding, wisdom and patience with others. They also generally have more time for and appreciation of relationships, including with grandchildren. Besides helping their grandchildren develop an appreciation for the past, active grand-parenting helps older adults avoid isolation and dependence, while finding additional meaning and purpose in life.

2. Reflection and Introspection

Adults at this stage tend to enjoy reflecting on past situations and experiences. While they may not do as well with short term memory, they tend to have less difficulty recalling names, places, emotions and lessons from long ago. They easily connect their past experiences and stories to present-day situations faced by others. Older adults can greatly add value to others through sharing the insight and wisdom they've gained from their life experiences, both good and bad.

Along with these qualities come several challenges...

1. Declining Health

With aging, comes physical decline, some of which may be due to lifestyle, such as poor diet and lack of exercise, rather than illness or the natural aging process. The experience of most as they age is that energy reserves dwindle and muscle mass decreases. Body systems and organs, such as the heart and lungs, become less efficient. The immune system is not as effective in guarding against disease. There is a proneness to ailments like arthritis, rheumatism, cancer, eye cataracts, dental problems, diabetes, hearing and vision problems, heart disease, hypertension, and orthopedic injuries. Older adults are also more prone to mental and emotional problems like depression, anxiety and dementia as well as conditions like Alzheimer's disease and strokes.

It's important to note that keeping mentally active and exercising regularly greatly improve one's quality of life during this season. Older adults who have kept their minds active and fit throughout their lifetime continue to learn and grow. Doing puzzles, having hobbies, learning to use a computer and reading are a few examples of activities that minimize the decline of memory and other cognitive functions. In addition, those who have kept physically active, remained fit and eaten wholesome foods tend to remain much stronger for longer than those who have not. This should be a lesson to younger adults who have an opportunity to modify their health habits early in life.

2. Retirement

People typically retire from their formal work roles in this season, which can lead to a drastic change in lifestyle. Work provides a sense of importance and place for many and the loss of that work can lead to negative psychological impact such as feelings of depression, uselessness and low self-esteem. Having hobbies, volunteering in charities and having other interests outside work will generally help a person retire better. In addition, if the person had not created opportunities to create passive income (income that is independent of my effort), then they will find it difficult to maintain the lifestyle they were once accustomed to. Things they took for granted like fueling the car, buying airtime to communicate, dressing well and living in a comfortable home may now not be automatic and older adults often find themselves in the uncomfortable position of having to rely on their adult children for their upkeep.

As I mentioned earlier, people are living longer and longer today. Those who retire while in good health, with financial freedom, good family and social networks and active hobbies or volunteer engagements usually look forward to retirement, where they can continue being productive at a more leisurely pace. As a young leader, it is thus important to ensure from an early age that you are being a good steward, paying yourself first by putting aside a portion of every income you earn towards future retirement. Also ensure that you have a life outside work, including time for people and hobbies.

What is the key task of this stage? One of the greatest things a person can do is structure their lives so that they can leave a legacy by passing on the wisdom they have gained over the years. They have an opportunity to become a sage, similar to the legendary Jedi Master Yoda, in the movie Star Wars. Respected for his age and wisdom, Yoda's main role in the film series is to coach other Jedi Masters. My favorite Yoda quote is 'Do. Or do not. There is no try'[36]. This is an invocation to a younger self-doubting leader to quit trying and just do it. Simple, but profound!

In the bible, the book of Psalms is a book of prayers and songs by several people, including King David. In one of them, David says the following prayer to God…

"My mouth will tell of your righteous deeds, of your saving acts all day long— though I know not how to relate them all. I will come and proclaim your mighty acts, Sovereign LORD; I will

36 From 'The Empire Strikes Back'

proclaim your righteous deeds, yours alone. Since my youth, God, you have taught me, and to this day I declare your marvelous deeds. Even when I am old and gray, do not forsake me, my God, till I declare your power to the next generation, your mighty acts to all who are to come"[37].

Here is the prayer of an older man who had been through many incredible experiences throughout his lifetime. His comfortable life as a young shepherd boy had been rocked when the famous prophet Samuel anointed him as the next king of Israel. On a trip to take supplies to his brothers who were in the army, he had killed the giant that had defied Israel's army for forty days. This had launched his career, first as a famous military general, then as a fugitive warlord and ultimately, as king over all of Israel. Under his watch, Israel had moved from being a small, cowering nation to a respected regional power.

David had also made his share of mistakes, including the terrible blunder of having an affair with the wife of one of his generals and then ordering for that general's assassination. He experienced major drama among his children and had survived a coup attempt by his own son. Through it all, David's greatest strength was his dependence on God. He repented when he made mistakes and actively sought God's help when he faced great challenges. The conclusion about his life, written centuries later, was that he fulfilled God's purpose for his generation throughout his lifetime.[38]

This man clearly had a lot to teach the next generation! Because of his experiences, he was well placed to help younger leaders see, not just what to do, but also what to avoid as they grew in their leadership. David, realizing this, prayed that God would

37 *Psalm. 71:15-18*
38 *Acts 13:36*

allow him to live long enough to declare God's power to the next generation, through sharing with them about the mighty acts of God that he had witnessed in his lifetime.

The season of reflection is an important season. Far from being a season of declining usefulness, it can be the leader's most effective season. That is, if they are in a place where they are positioned to nurture and mentor next generation leaders. I have seen some older professors who have had tremendous impact by intentionally mentoring students, going way farther than just classroom instruction. I know several older couples who have opened up their homes to younger couples who receive mentorship and encouragement in their own marriages. One such couple opened a retreat center where younger leaders can come and spend time resting and also receiving mentorship from them. I also know some older business leaders who are adding great value to the organizations on whose boards they serve.

One of my mentors is Bedan Mbugua, who is popularly known as Mr. B. Although in his seventies, he is extremely active and involved in different initiatives to add value to others. He mentors younger leaders who are giving national leadership in his areas of passion, which include environmental conservation and food security. He has a passion for gardening and we enjoy visiting his beautiful garden. He runs a weekly exercise class for older adults to help them lead an active lifestyle and learn about good nutrition. And he is quite physically fit, jumping rope and riding his bike in a way that would astound many younger leaders! There is never a dull moment around Mr. B and he's always surrounded by younger leaders that he is adding value to.

One of the struggles older adults often face is loneliness and isolation, but this need not be the case, as they avail themselves to add value to others. Your role as a sage in this season will provide you with a sense of purpose, as you see God use your experiences to bless younger leaders. It will also provide you with a sense of community. On a recent trip, I met a couple in their sixties from Australia who were mentors to several younger leaders who are in their mid-thirties. They were so committed to these friendships that they had travelled halfway across the world to support an initiative these young leaders had put together. I marveled as I saw what a blessing they were to these they were mentoring, but also how much energy and joy being around these young leaders had brought into their lives in the process.

It's important, even in this season, to commit to continue being curious and open to learning new things. Leaders at this stage are well served by learning to ask questions from those younger than them so as to understand their context and issues better. Being a lifelong learner will help you stay in touch with the reality of those you are mentoring and allow the wisdom you share to be contextual and relevant to those who receive it.

For Carol and I, we desire that God willing, we will continue to be a blessing to others during our years of reflection. Our vision is to have a retreat center where we will regularly host couples in ministry leadership from across the world for a time of rejuvenation, care and mentoring. We believe our experience and wisdom will be a blessing to them and that by spending time with them, we will continue to add value to the expansion of God's kingdom, until He calls us home!

IN CONCLUSION

Throughout this volume, we have examined the seasons of a leader's life. You've probably realized by now that to live a life of maximum effectiveness and impact calls for great intentionality by a leader, whatever season of life they are currently in. One of the greatest kings the ancient nation of Israel ever had was undoubtedly King David. Many centuries after David's death, one of the New Testament writers, Dr. Luke, had this observation to make about him.

"Now when David had served God's purpose in his own generation, he fell asleep; he was buried with his ancestors and his body decayed"[39].

I love it! The man was not only an effective military and political leader who brought peace, wealth and security to his nation. In the process of his career, we are told that He served his God-given purpose in his own generation. And only after he had served this had he come to the end of his life. What a great epitaph. If only these words could be written about every one of us by the end of our life!

When we as leaders fail to understand that there is an even bigger season ahead for us, then we plateau in our leadership. We get stuck in one stage and fail to build the foundations to move effectively to the next. That's why many founders refuse to raise other leaders, to transition to the next leadership stage and end up stifling the organizations that they lead.

39 Acts 13:36

My prayer in writing this book is that through understanding the seasons of leadership, many government, corporate, business, church and family leaders will gain a long term view of leadership that will result in healthier nations, organizations, churches and families!

God bless,
Muriithi

BIBLIOGRAPHY

Barnes, Robert E. Ready for Responsibility: How to Equip Your Children for Work and Marriage. Grand Rapids, MI: Zondervan, 1997.

Brotherson, Sean E. Understanding Brain Development in Young Children. Extension Bulletin FS-609. NDSU Extension Service, North Dakota State University, Fargo, ND, 2005, April.

Clinton, Robert J. The Making of A Leader: Recognizing the Lessons and Stages of Leadership Development. Colorado Springs, CO: NavPress, 1988.

Collins, Gary R. Christian Counseling: A Comprehensive Guide. Nashville, TN: Thomas Nelson, 1980.

Erikson, Eric. Childhood And Society. London, United Kingdom: Vintage Books, 1995.

Maxwell, John C. The 21 Most Powerful Minutes in A Leader's Day. Nashville, TN: Thomas Nelson, Inc., 2000.

Monroe, Myles. Becoming A Leader: Everyone Can Do It. Lanham, MD: Pneuma Life, 1993.

Stanley, Andy. Next Generation Leader. Colorado Springs, CO: Multnomah Books, 2003

Stanley, Andy, Joiner, Reggie & Jones, Lane. Seven Practices of Effective Ministry. Colorado Springs, CO: Multnomah Books, 2004.

Stanley, Andy. Visioneering. Colorado Springs, CO: Multnomah Books, 2016.

Winter, Bruce W. "Acts and Food Shortages." In The Book of Acts in its Graeco-Roman Setting. Edited by David W. J. Gill and Conrad Gempf. Grand Rapids, MI: Eerdmans, 1994.

Made in the
USA
Monee, IL

13768591R00053